SCIENTIFIC COLLABORATION

Pierre and Marie CURIE

The Couple Who Pioneered Radioactivity Research

Lisa Idzikowski

ROSEN PUBLISHING

Published in 2021 by The Rosen Publishing Group, Inc.
29 East 21st Street, New York, NY 10010

Library of Congress Cataloging-in-Publication Data

Names: Idzikowski, Lisa, author.
Title: Pierre and Marie Curie : the couple who pioneered radioactivity research / Lisa Idzikowski.
Description: New York : Rosen Publishing, 2021. | Series: Scientific collaboration | Audience: Grades 7 to 12. | Includes bibliographical references and index.
Identifiers: LCCN 2019013889 | ISBN 9781725342385 (library bound) | ISBN 9781725342378 (pbk.)
Subjects: LCSH: Curie, Marie, 1867-1934—Juvenile literature. | Curie, Pierre, 1859-1906—Juvenile literature. | Chemists—Poland—Biography—Juvenile literature. | Chemists—France—Biography—Juvenile literature. | Radioactivity—History—Juvenile literature. | Discoveries in science—Juvenile literature.
Classification: LCC QD22.C8 I39 2021 | DDC 540.92/2 [B] —dc23
LC record available at https://lccn.loc.gov/2019013889

Printed in the United States of America

Photo Credits: Cover, pp. 17, 21, 22–23 Roger Viollet Collection/Getty Images (Pierre Curie), cover, pp. 3, 30–31 AFP/Getty Images (Marie Curie); pp. 7, 32 Everett Historical/Shutterstock.com; pp. 11, 46, 54–55, 58–59 Print Collector/Hulton Archive/Getty Images; pp. 13, 16 Universal Images Group/Getty Images; p. 25 Science & Society Picture Library/Getty Images; p. 29 NLM/Science Source; p. 35 Science Source; p. 36 De Agostini Picture Library/Getty Images; p. 38 BlueRingMedia/Shutterstock.com; pp. 40–41 Emilio Segrè Visual Archives/American Institute of Physics/Science Source; p. 44 London Express/Hulton Archive/Getty Images; pp. 50–51 Bettmann/Getty Images; p. 53 Vector FX/Shutterstock.com; p. 62 FPG/Archive Photos/Getty Images; pp. 66–67 Mark_Kostich/Shutterstock.com.

CPSIA Compliance Information: Batch #BSR20. For further information contact Rosen Publishing, New York, New York at 1-800-237-9932.

Pierre and Marie CURIE

The Couple Who Pioneered Radioactivity Research

CONTENTS

Introduction

In the nineteenth century, many scientific discoveries graced the world scene. Scientists explored South America and the Galapagos Islands, experimented with electricity, and pondered the structure of the atom. Inventors fashioned the telegraph and then the telephone. People traveled by train, and steamships sailed across the Atlantic Ocean. And a new term—dinosaur—described ancient unearthed fossils.[1]

Two dynamic scientists-to-be were born in the middle of this exciting century: Pierre Curie in Paris, France, and Marie Sklodowska Curie in Warsaw, Poland. By sheer luck, both individuals came through an early life in countries not far removed from political revolutions. They grew up in loving families, obtained educations, and went to college at the Sorbonne in France. At about this time, two scientific discoveries of unusual "rays" swept the world. These new rays became the talk among scientists. Ordinary people wondered how X-rays could penetrate skin to reveal bones underneath. Pierre and Marie marveled at the Becquerel rays. They decided that Marie would investigate this phenomenon.

Marie Sklodowska Curie and Pierre Curie shared a great love for science and formed a dynamic partnership of scientific experimentation.

Marie jumped into her research and quickly uncovered unexpected results. Pierre decided to put his scientific work aside and team up with his wife. This was the beginning of their great partnership in science. Together, the Curies brought to life two entirely new elements: polonium and radium. Their scientific progress shone around the world and brought both happiness and grief. Pierre disliked attention. Fame was impossible to avoid after the Curies were awarded the Nobel Prize.

Partnerships are challenging. The one between Pierre and Marie was no different—they each had faults, but their collaboration and the scientific work they produced together was truly great.

Unfortunately for science and the world, fate dealt a cruel hand to the couple who loved science and each other. Pierre suffered a horrendous accident and died young. How could Marie go on? Devastated and depressed, she did. As a single parent and scientist, Marie accomplished much throughout the rest of her life. She continued her research on the discovery she coined "radioactivity." She became the first person to be awarded a second Nobel Prize. When World War I came to France, Marie volunteered. Her mobile X-ray–equipped vehicles saved many lives.

After the war, Marie concentrated on her laboratory. She wanted it to be the best place for scientific research about radioactivity, and she wished it to continue after she was dead and gone. Marie guided her daughters and watched them develop. One became a scientist, and in many ways she was just like her father. The other became an accomplished pianist and author. Marie kept up with the scientific world. She made the Radium Institute into a world-class research institution for medical research and physical science. Marie also saw scientists build on her earlier work and struggle through their own experimentation and discoveries. Eventually, the age of atomic science had arrived.

Years after her death, both she and Pierre received a great honor. Their physical remains were transferred to the Pantheon in Paris, the final resting place of France's greatest citizens.

CHAPTER ONE

The Early Years

One minute, four-year-old Manya effortlessly read a sentence from her sister's book, and the next, she burst into sobs. Why did her parents seem surprised? Were they upset? Had she done something wrong? No. Manya's parents didn't know that she could read. She was only four.[1]

Young Maria Sklodowska

Maria Salomea Sklodowska, nicknamed Manya (and later known as Marie Curie), was born into a loving family of four siblings on a late autumn day, November 7, 1867. She joined her sisters, Zosia, six years old; Bronia, three; and Helena, eighteen months; along with her brother Jozef, four.[2] Both of Manya's parents taught school, and the family lived in an apartment connected to the school where her mother served as headmistress.

The city of Warsaw, where Manya was born, felt far different than her loving family. No longer did it stand as part of the country of Poland. By the end of the eighteenth century, Poland had been taken over by Russia, Austria, and Prussia.[3] It no longer existed as an official country. Maps showed it instead as Vistula Land. The

Wladyslaw Sklodowski sits for a photo with his daughters Marie, Bronia, and Helena (*from left to right*).

Names in Poland

In Poland, parents usually gave their children nicknames. In Marie's family, Zosia was short for Sophie, Bronia for Bronislawa, Hela for Helena, and Jozio for Jozef. Marie had three nicknames: Manya, Manyusya, and Anciupecio. Also, last names had different spellings according to gender. As a woman, Marie's name was Sklodowska, with an "a" at the end. Men used an "i" instead of an "a," so her father was a Sklodowski. For mixed-gender groups, the "i" form is used. This practice is still used by many Polish people today.

Polish people had bravely fought in two different revolts. They tried to take back their country. Many died in the failed attempts. Others were sent away to Siberian prisons in cold northern Russia. Because of all this turmoil, Russia sought revenge. The Russian government vowed to stamp out everything that had been Polish. Speaking Polish was against the law. Reading Polish books and practicing the culture was forbidden. And learning Polish was not allowed in school.

The Polish people couldn't successfully fight with weapons. They found other ways to battle back. Manya's parents and many other teachers stood up against the Russian laws. This happened at home or secretly in school. Polish culture, language, religion, and literature were taught and kept alive. At home, Manya's mother played the piano and sang songs about Polish heroes.[4] Her father recited Polish poetry and read books aloud, speaking in Polish. He also taught his children about the worlds he loved best: science and math. One of Manya's favorite places at home was her father's study, or workroom. It was filled with scientific

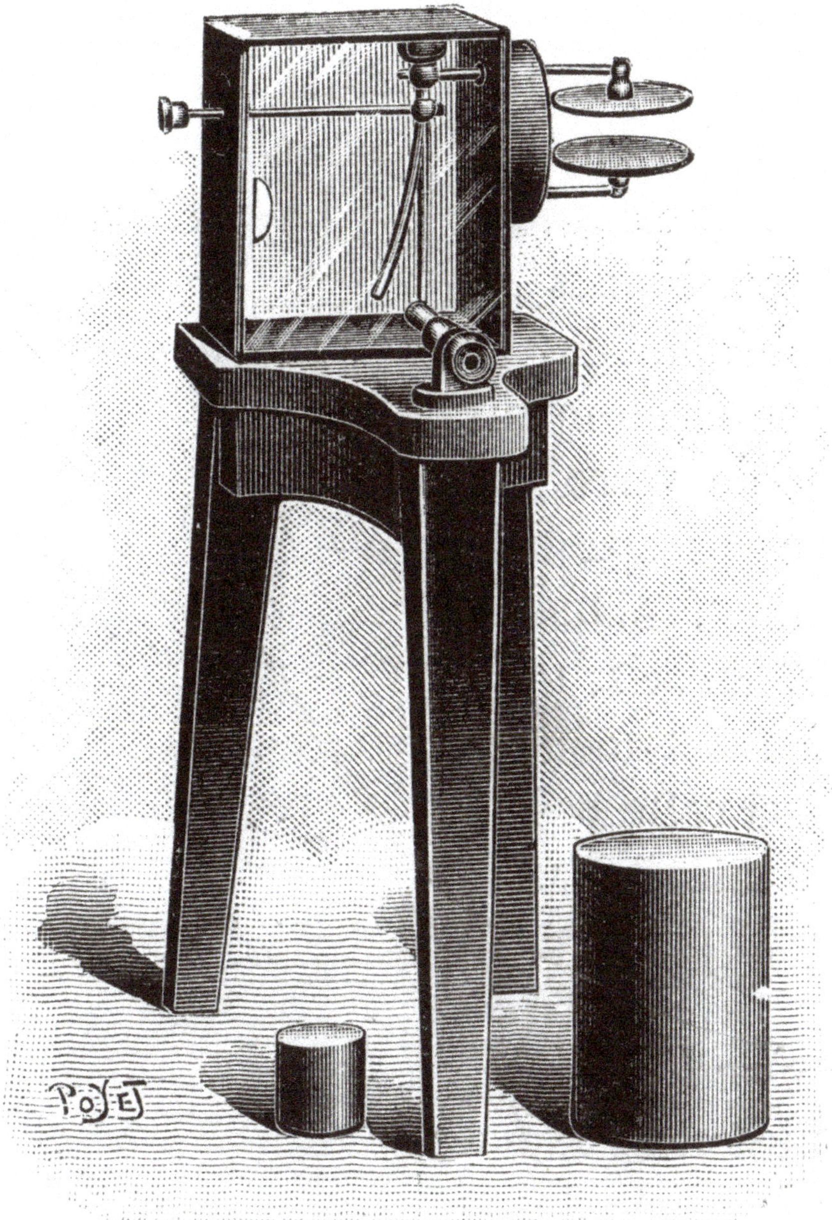

As a couple, the Curies were inspired by their childhood upbringings in loving, inventive families. They designed and used this electroscope in their radioactivity research.

tools. A barometer hung on one wall, and she loved the glass case crowded with tubes, scales, mineral specimens, and a very special instrument, an electroscope.[5]

Manya had a talent for remembering things, both good and bad. Her father's special instruments filled her with good feelings. She also suffered several extreme challenges as a young girl. When Manya was nine, her beloved older sister Zosia caught typhus. It was a horrible disease that took her life.

Almost a year later, young Manya left home for boarding school. Here she played a part in the secretive schooling practiced by some Polish teachers. Manya was so smart. She knew history, literature, German, French, Polish, and Russian, all better than her schoolmates. So, when the secret signal bell—two long, then two short rings—sounded in school one day, Manya and her class jumped into action. All the Polish books and papers disappeared. The room changed into a proper Russian classroom with twenty-five girls practicing their sewing. Ten-year-old Manya, dressed in her navy-blue school uniform, performed for the Russian inspector. She recited a religious prayer and answered questions about Russian rulers—all in perfect Russian! Manya's performance pleased the inspector. The pretending worked. The inspector left, not realizing that right before he showed up the class had been studying and learning about Polish history in their forbidden Polish language. Their secret was safe! Afterward, Manya was probably proud of herself, but she burst into tears.[6]

How could Manya manage another hardship? She and her siblings knew their mother had been sick for a long time. She was always coughing and never hugged or kissed anyone. No successful medical treatment existed for tuberculosis. Now, just over two years after Zosia died, their mother was very ill. Her mother's death was a terrible blow for Manya. It took many months for her to recover even a bit. When her father sent her to a Russian school, she wondered why at first. Eventually, Manya understood. She needed to earn a diploma. Only the Russian schools could award them. After working hard through the years, much like high school today, Manya graduated on June 12, 1883. She had not only done well but graduated first in her class.

Young Pierre Curie

Pierre Curie loved nature and being in the country. Every chance he got, he would head for the nearest forest, field, or pond. Pierre observed birds and dragonflies, hunted for salamanders, and caught frogs and tritons.[7] Pierre's older brother, Jacques, often joined in the fun. With no other siblings, the two brothers became best friends as they grew up.

Pierre Curie was born on May 15, 1859, in Paris, France. His parents and three-and-a-half-year-old brother were happy to add another member to their family. Dr. Eugène Curie and his family lived near the Natural History Museum, where he worked. Mrs. Claire Curie worked to make their home comfortable for everyone.

While growing up, Pierre witnessed many curious matters. His medical doctor father believed in helping anyone who needed assistance. This included everyday working families. At certain times, this caused difficulties. During periods of protest and unrest in France, Dr. Curie found himself on the side of the protesters. Could twelve-year-old Pierre make sense of his father helping rebel soldiers? Perhaps not. Still, the Curie brothers helped their father as he aided the wounded.[8] Pierre also saw his father's intense interest in the natural world. Dr. Curie observed, identified, and collected plants and animals in nearby areas. He would have preferred to do independent research in science. But how could he support his family? Dr. Curie found jobs that used

Pierre Curie grew up in a happy family of four. In this photo, Pierre is standing behind his father. His brother, Jacques, stands beside him, and his mother sits beside her husband.

his talent as a medical doctor. His two boys shared his interest in plants and animals and his love of nature.

Interestingly, Pierre didn't attend elementary school. From a young age, Pierre's parents could see that their youngest son learned in a different way. His mother, father, and brother tutored him at home. He learned all about geometry, chemistry, physics, and biology from his family. His father's large home library was put to good use.[9] It was there that Pierre taught himself all about history and literature. Around age fourteen, this comfortable routine changed. Dr. Curie hired a tutor. Pierre began studying with Professor Bazille, who helped him advance in math and

A lover of nature, Pierre Curie's father worked at the French National Museum of Natural History.

Latin. This situation suited both the professor and student. Studies went so well that about two years later, Pierre was far enough along that he enrolled at the Sorbonne, Paris's premier college.[10]

CHAPTER TWO

Young Scientists

Fifteen-year-old Manya had every reason to be pleased at her graduation. She carried on the family tradition of doing well in school, measuring up to her sister and brother who graduated before her. She also proudly accepted the gold medal for finishing first in her class. Not surprisingly, some unpleasant feelings marked the day too. What would she do with her life now? And how long would the painfully sad memories of her dear mother linger?

Manya Strikes Out on Her Own

Manya's father sensed her distress. Was it sadness, uncertainty, or exhaustion? According to the customs of the time, Manya now had three choices: she could get married; she could teach in a local school; or she could go away to college in Paris or Saint Petersburg, Russia. Manya longed for an advanced education, but her family had little money.[1] Her father made a decision. Manya would stay with her relatives to the south. Away from school. Away from studies. Away from the city.

With her faithful dog Lancet, Manya traveled by train and horse-drawn cart. She rode south to the country estates owned by various relatives. What sweet times lay ahead! Manya filled her days with cousins and play—anything but studying and school subjects. She took long hikes, played games, swam, fished, and rode horses. The *kulig*, or sleigh party, became one of Manya's favorite activities.[2] She loved the costumes, the music, and the dancing. Manya wrote home describing fun nights of food, nice-looking young men, and music that played on and on. At one kulig, she told how they danced the last dance at eight o'clock the next morning![3] When summer arrived, Manya and her sister Hela were invited to stay at another country house. This time, they journeyed north to stay with one of their mother's former students. Both girls had a wonderful time before traveling back to Warsaw.

Manya was well rested. But what was next? She had her eyes on attending a university, but two very big obstacles blocked the way. The University of Warsaw still did not allow women, and her family still lacked money. The would-be scholar tackled the problem. She offered herself as a tutor for math and French and joined another secret school, the "Floating University," which gave lessons in anatomy, natural history, and sociology.[4] By the days and months, Manya gained knowledge, but hardly any money.

Always struggling forward, Manya hatched a plan to help get herself and Bronia to a university in Paris. Both girls wished to attend the Sorbonne. Here's how they could manage, according to Manya. Bronia would go first and become a doctor, as she wanted. Then, she would pay for Manya to go. Where would the initial money come from? Easy, Manya insisted. She would get a job as a governess. It paid a lot more money than tutoring and included essentially free living.

In the countryside of rural Poland, the *kulig*, or sleigh party, was a favorite winter activity.

By January 1, 1886, eighteen-year-old Manya boarded the train for her second post as governess. Roughly seven hours later, she arrived in the country town of Szczuki and the home of her employer. As might be expected, Manya worked hard and tutored two of the family's children. She also enjoyed country walks, skating in the winter, and the summer flower garden. Her duties left time for her reading. Books on physics, sociology, and anatomy and physiology filled nighttime hours. All seemed well until the eldest son came home from school. Manya was in for a huge surprise—Casimir fell in love and asked her to marry him.

Unfortunately, the happiness did not last. Manya's employers refused to let the couple marry. They argued that she was a poor governess, and that as a son of a well-to-do farm manager, Casimir could make a better match. It was another blow to Manya. And she couldn't leave her job because Bronia depended on the money she sent every month. Although terribly sad and angry, Manya stuck it out. She pretended to be fine and started tutoring local peasant children in Polish. She didn't care that it could have landed her in prison. Determined, Manya also learned a bit of basic chemistry from a chemist at the farm's factory. Both activities gave her satisfaction and pleasure.

Finally, after about six years spent in assorted houses as governess, Manya had enough. While back home and again attending the Floating University, she discovered the wonder of working in a laboratory. She had a knack for experimental work in chemistry and physics. Then her big break came. Twenty-three-year old Manya left for Paris. She didn't like saying goodbye to her father, but she promised to return from university studies in two or three years. He wished his youngest good luck.[5]

She changed her name to Marie Sklodowska when she registered for the fall session at the Sorbonne. She would now be able to freely speak her once forbidden language. She would

This view overlooks the Sorbonne in Paris, 1880.

Changeable Atoms

When Marie started her research, little was known about atoms. Scientists believed that atoms were solid chunks of material and unchangeable. She found that uranium emitted rays constantly. Nothing she did—changing the temperature, smashing it into tiny pieces, or adding liquid—changed the behavior of uranium's rays. Marie reasoned that the emission of rays was an atomic property. And that meant that the ideas about atoms changed.

now be able to learn math and physics from master professors. She would now be able to conduct experiments in scientific laboratories. Marie was in heaven! Everything she had dreamed of was happening. She took full advantage of the experience, and by July 1893, Marie completed her classes. Not surprisingly, she racked up another "first" in her life. This time, it was first place for a master's degree in physics. By the next year, Marie had not only earned her second master's degree in math, she had also been selected to investigate the magnetic properties of steel—her first real experimental research. Little did she know that it would lead to an enormous life change.

Pierre Dives In

Sixteen-year-old Pierre excelled in his studies at the Sorbonne. Two years of study netted him a master's degree in physics. Instead of continuing his studies, he helped with finances at home. The brilliant student accepted a job and began working as an assistant for the Sorbonne's physics labs. His brother, Jacques, already worked there in the Department of Mineralogy, so this seemed natural. Pierre's fondness for nature had not stopped. Wandering among the woods and admiring the plants and foliage gave him a refuge from the city. He also fell in love with a childhood acquaintance.

Tragedy struck. It is not known how his young love died, but she did, and Pierre blamed himself. He could not forgive or forget, so he guarded against falling in love with any other young woman. Could he live like this forever? Pierre tried. He dedicated all his energy to scientific experimentation. Before long, he and Jacques dove into experiments that examined crystals and the effect of electric fields. They made some startling discoveries together and presented papers on this effect, then dubbed piezoelectricity.[6]

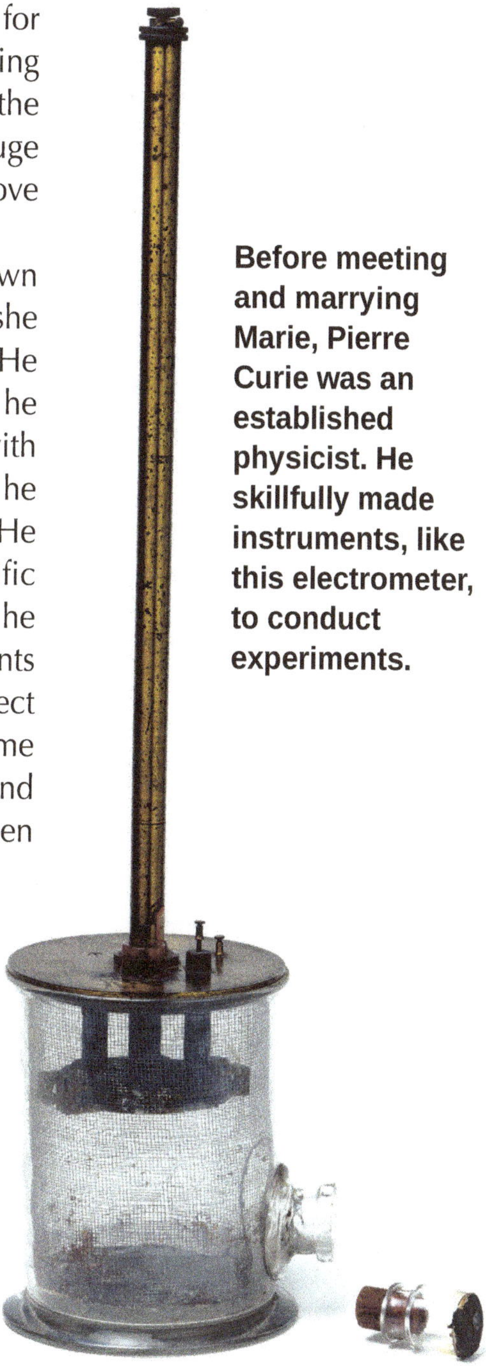

Before meeting and marrying Marie, Pierre Curie was an established physicist. He skillfully made instruments, like this electrometer, to conduct experiments.

Pierre assumed more responsibility when he took charge of the laboratory of the new School of Industrial Physics and Chemistry of the City of Paris. Besides teaching many students, directing a lab, and gaining a small space to conduct his own experiments, he soon met Marie Sklodowska.[7]

CHAPTER THREE

Together at Last

Marie Sklodowska was dedicated to her studies and science. She showered her affections on two things: her family and her beloved Poland. Pierre Curie was dedicated to his students, scientific research, and work. He offered his affections to his father, mother, and brother. Both Marie and Pierre had dismissed the idea of love for a husband or wife.

At First Sight

Was it love at first sight? Perhaps for Pierre, but not for Marie. Pierre had his students, lab duties, and independent research at the School of Industrial Physics and Chemistry of the City of Paris, the EPCI. At thirty-five, he lived comfortably with his parents in Sceaux, a small city near Paris. During the summer, his brother would visit, and together the two brother scientists would continue their coexperiments and discoveries.[1]

Marie was consumed with finishing her coursework and studies in order to qualify for her second degree in mathematics. She had begun her assigned independent research project on the magnetic properties of steel. The only major difficulty at this point was that Marie needed more space to conduct her research. What could she do? Where could she go for adequate space?

A surprising coincidence cropped up. A visiting professor from Poland who knew Marie suggested that she come for tea.

Was it fate or chance that brought Marie and Pierre together in the spring of 1894?[2] Pierre had already arrived before Marie appeared. At first glance, Marie immediately saw a tall man standing near a window. She imagined him to be young, and his smile attracted her. Pierre noticed a serious attitude in Marie's ash-gray eyes and quiet speech.[3] A friendly conversation began and flowed between the two young scientists. Both came from families invested in education. Both had fathers interested in science. And in both families, wealth was scarce. Friendly small talk changed to scientific discussion. Pierre was amazed. Could this be true? He talked about the science he loved with a young woman who understood his technical language and excitement. He spoke of his research on crystals and magnetism. At the same time, Marie asked thoughtful questions and gave insightful comments. She told him of her upcoming exams and her search for laboratory space. Marie also spoke of her dedication to Poland, her father, and plans to return to Warsaw to become a teacher.

A Promise

Marie and Pierre saw each other several times over the next few months at meetings of the Physics Society in a lab at the Sorbonne and in Marie's apartment. Pierre had once written in his diary that women in science were rare. Now, he had fallen in love and sensed that he had to act. He asked Marie to marry him. She did not respond with his hoped-for answer. Instead, she left to visit her family in Poland. Pierre felt that Marie was meant to be with him. His sadness turned to joy when she wrote to him only ten days later.

Pierre didn't hesitate. He answered Marie, asking again if she planned on coming back in the fall. He poured out his dreams of the two of them working together on scientific projects. Again and again Pierre wrote, imploring her to come back to Paris in the fall. At one point, he suggested that they live in an apartment together, one that he had already seen, which had a nice garden. In early autumn, Marie sent a letter containing two things: a picture of herself and the magic words. She would come back to Paris! Pierre's heart swelled. Surely now she would agree to marry him. Ever the industrious student, Marie again held off. Pierre became desperate. He offered Marie an outlandish proposal. They could move together to Poland, and he would give French lessons if she would agree to marry. Her answer was still no.

In the spirit of deepening feelings, Pierre took Marie to meet his parents. She, in turn, convinced him to write up his research about magnetism. He successfully defended his thesis, received a PhD, and became a professor. Marie could no longer refuse and accepted her Pierre. On a beautiful day, July 26, 1895, Pierre and Marie took the train to Sceaux. Close family and friends met them at the town hall. After a simple wedding ceremony, the party walked to Pierre's house. Roses and irises filled the garden as everyone dined on turkey and peaches.[4] Mr. and Mrs. Curie left on their honeymoon not by car or train, but by bicycle. They had purchased and outfitted themselves with new bikes for a trip along the coast bicycling from one fishing village to the next.

Their happy honeymoon ended, and the newlyweds began a life together in an apartment in Paris. Marie juggled her new responsibilities. Pierre helped a bit, but most of the new tasks fell on Marie. She managed the shopping, kept track of expenses, and learned to cook. She also completed her research project on

France's premier scientific couple poses for a photograph not long after they married.

Early in 1904, Marie, Pierre, and their firstborn daughter, Irène, are captured in a photo sharing a moment together.

steel and earned a certificate to teach at a women's school. Life went on beautifully for the couple. When Marie learned she would have a baby, she was thrilled. She didn't appreciate feeling sick, but she made the best of it. In September 1897, Irène was born. Great happiness lasted until about two weeks later, when Pierre's mother died from cancer. Pierre wouldn't dream of Marie giving up her scientific work. She was happy but overwhelmed. A perfect solution came to mind. Why not ask Dr. Curie to move in with them?

Pierre's father agreed instantly. He moved with his proud son and daughter-in-law to a house on the edge of Paris. How wonderful it would be to care for his cute granddaughter. And Marie could feel confident that while she was at the lab, an ideal babysitter watched over her child.

The Big Decision

With everything under control, Marie took the next big step. No woman in the world had up to this point earned a doctorate degree in science.[5] Pierre agreed that she should start working immediately. But what would she do? Marie knew that a PhD required original research. She already spent long hours in the lab and worked at home late into the night. She had to find a subject to investigate. Marie studied the latest scientific

Some Mysterious Rays

At first, Wilhelm Röntgen couldn't believe what he was seeing. He shut himself in his lab and worked to confirm his findings. What were these mysterious rays that could see through wood and skin and take pictures of people's bones? It was thrilling and scary. The discovery of X-rays caught the attention of people. After announcing his discovery in 1895, other scientists scrambled to experiment with this unusual phenomenon.

In 1901, German physicist Wilhelm Röntgen was awarded the first Nobel Prize in Physics.

journals. What looked interesting? What could she start on without too much preparation? Of course. She thought about the rather new discoveries of two types of energy: X-rays and Becquerel rays. X-rays had been discovered in 1895. Becquerel rays, which proved most important to Marie's later studies, had been discovered in 1896 by Henri Becquerel. These rays were emitted from uranium salts. They didn't require the presence of light to emit. Scientists and the world went crazy over X-rays. However, Becquerel rays didn't capture the imagination of many—except Marie.[6]

CHAPTER FOUR

Radioactive

Marie was hooked and Pierre was intrigued. Marie charged ahead on her quest to be the first woman in the world to earn a doctorate degree in science. Becquerel's rays would get her there, and Pierre would provide unfailing support. But where would she set up a lab?

An Old Storeroom

If Marie was disappointed, she didn't despair. The old, leaky, cold storeroom with wooden worktables and broken-down chairs would have to do. In December 1897, Marie moved ahead with her plans and experimental questions. What caused Becquerel rays? How did the rays make the surrounding air into a conductor of electricity? Could she measure the power Becquerel rays had to ionize the air? Marie had her lab, her questions, and her sample materials to test and observe. And she had Pierre's full support. Now, she needed instruments to carry out her investigations. She didn't have to go far for those; in fact, the equipment was all in the family. Two earlier inventions of physicists she knew and loved—her husband Pierre and brother-in-law Jacques—were perfect. She would use their Curie electrometer and piezoelectric quartz! These instruments formed the backbone of her tools. An ionization chamber built by Pierre completed the experimental setup. Marie began measuring the faint electrical currents in the ray-charged air.[1]

Marie quickly came to two conclusions. The intensity of the rays depended upon the amount of uranium contained in the tested sample, and introducing variables didn't matter. The

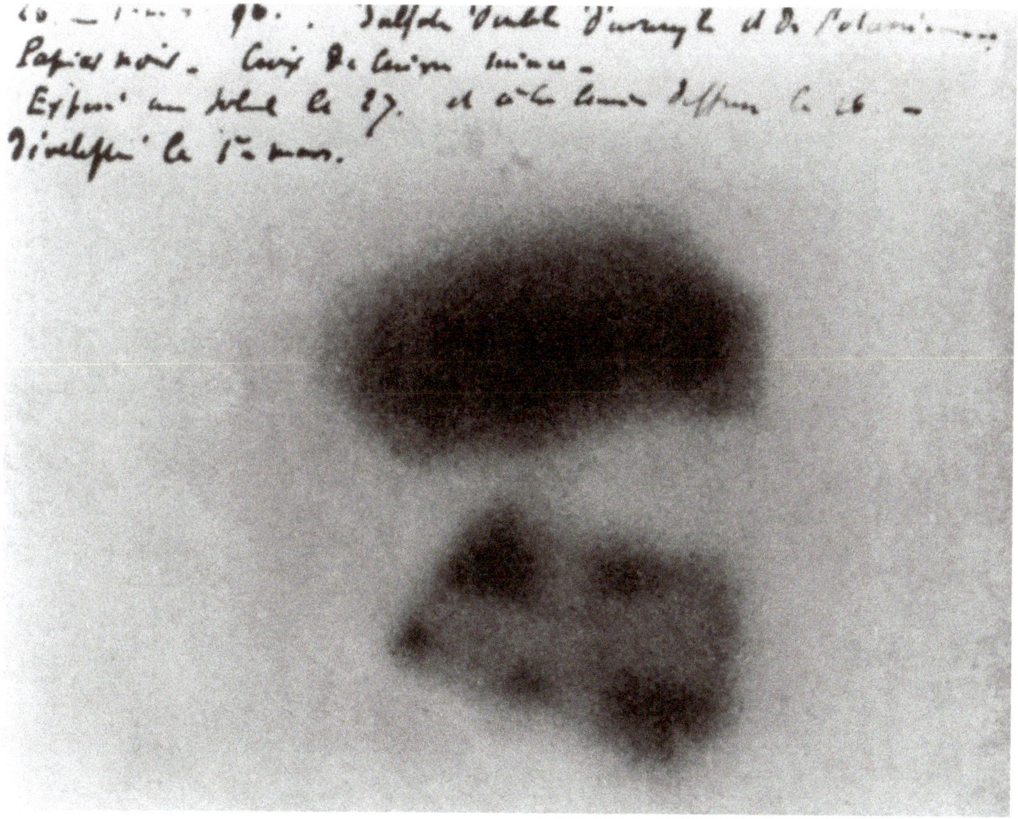

Physicist Henri Becquerel kept extensive notes (such as those at the top of this photo) as he experimented with uranium salts. The name "Becquerel rays" was given to the strange phenomenon that he discovered.

temperature and lighting, and the state of the sample, whether wet, dry, pulverized, or solid, made no difference. That was a big deal! Marie reasoned that the rays' ability to electrify the air was an atomic property of uranium.[2] Always the scientist and full of questions, Marie moved on. Was uranium the only element capable of emitting rays? Pierre helped get samples of other known elements of the time. On a February day in 1898, she tested thirteen elements, including copper and gold. None gave off any rays.[3] Marie kept testing different samples, and one day, she received surprising results. When she tested pitchblende, a dark mineral compound, it produced an electrical current

Pitchblende is a dark mineral compound with radioactive properties.

four times stronger than expected.[4] Had she made a mistake? She remained calm and did more testing. Over and over, her results stayed the same. Some days later, she tried another mineral. Chalcolite, which contains thorium instead of uranium, also registered a high amount of conductivity. This meant that Becquerel's rays were not a phenomenon of uranium alone. By spring, Marie was ready to share her findings. She published her first research paper, "Rays Emitted by Compounds of Uranium and of Thorium."[5]

Quest for the New Element

Marie had tested all the known elements and other metals, metallic compounds, salts, and minerals. Minerals containing uranium and thorium gave off the mysterious rays. Then there was pitchblende—and it proved to be a bombshell! Marie sensed that something new and yet undiscovered lay deep within its dark mineral depths. Pierre agreed. Up until this time, he had helped Marie here and there. Now, he put aside his own research. Pierre's crystals would have to wait. The dynamic duo became full-time partners.

Convinced that a new element waited to be found, the Curies brought in another scientist. In physics, they were king and queen, but to break down pitchblende, they needed an experienced chemist. Gustave Bemont (1857–1937) joined and advised the team. The chemical separations and testing took many days and many trials. Exciting results followed! Sure enough, Marie and Pierre found the new element lurking among bismuth, a breakdown product of pitchblende. Their July 1898 research paper announced it: "On a New Radioactive Substance Contained in Pitchblende." With a radioactivity level about four hundred times greater than uranium, polonium, after Marie's

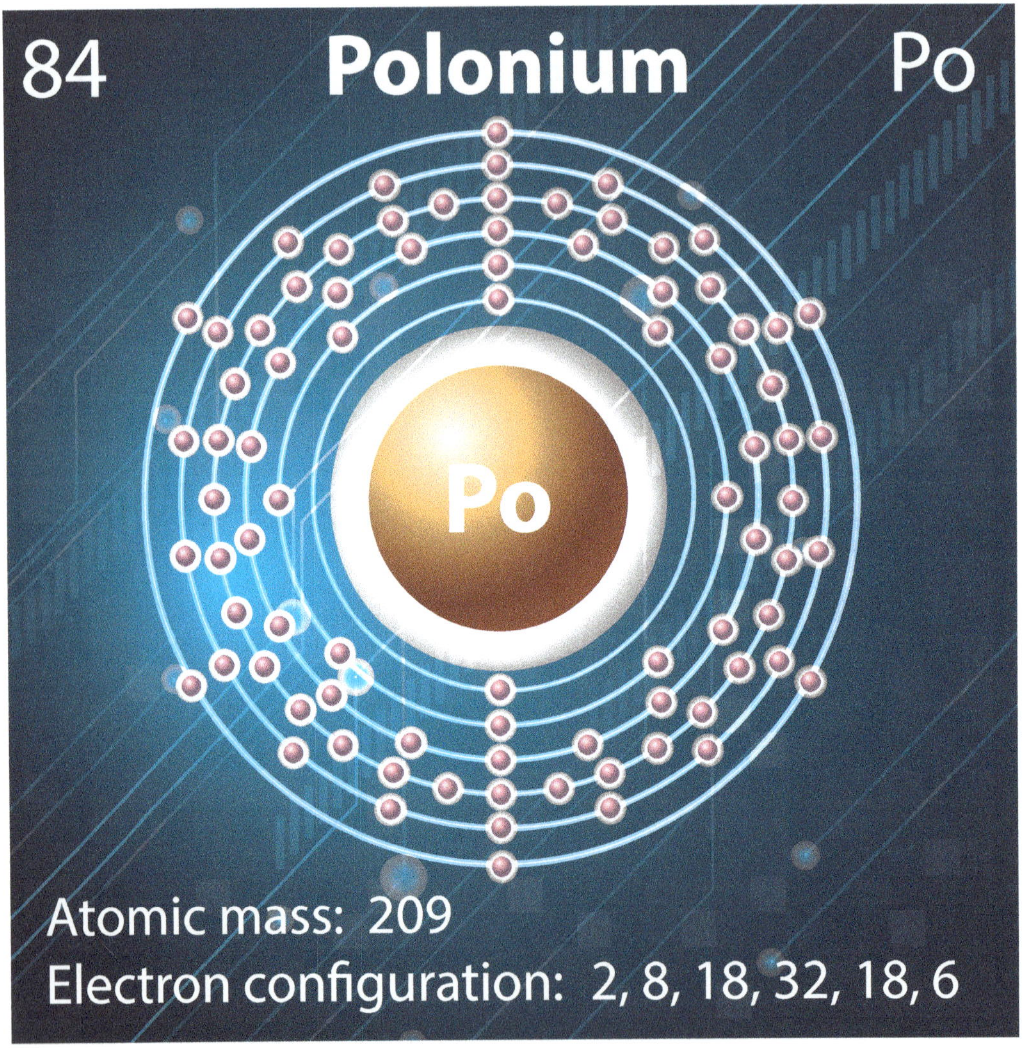

The radioactive element polonium is illustrated in this diagram. In the periodic table of elements, polonium has the atomic symbol "Po" and an atomic number of 84.

homeland of Poland, became the name of their new element. And scientists everywhere began using the new term "radioactive."[6]

Not Finished Yet

After a short summer vacation, the Curies tackled another round of chemical separations and testing. Their hunches proved correct. Another element presented itself among pitchblende's breakdown products. This time it was hiding in barium, and it outshone polonium. It tested out a whopping nine hundred times more radioactive than uranium.[7] What's more, a specialized chemical process confirmed that the Curies had identified another new element. They named it radium.

People took notice of the couple's scientific work. The French Academy of Sciences awarded its Gegner Prize to Marie. Other chemists spoke up. They needed actual physical specimens of the new elements. Did Marie and Pierre grumble? No, they attacked the problem, searching for a large supply of pitchblende and a bigger workspace.

Tons and tons of pitchblende arrived. Sacks of brown rock mixed with pine needles were dumped near Marie's new lab. The shed had once been used by medical students for dissecting bodies. Now, it was Marie's. Chemical separations started anew. Huge boiling vats stirred by Marie slowly unleashed their secrets. She concentrated on producing a sample of pure radium. Pierre experimented with the radioactive barium. Marie got closer and closer. Pierre found out that his samples could produce burns on the skin. Other scientists and doctors wished to do their own experiments and asked the Curies for help. Marie and Pierre never hesitated to share.

Word continued to spread about the couple's achievements. Soon, the University at Geneva in Switzerland tried to woo the Curies from France. Switzerland promised better lab space, better university positions, and better pay. The Curies said no when the Sorbonne increased their current pay and bettered their teaching positions.

Work never stopped in the shed. Its glass tube–filled benches and shelves contained various mixtures of radioactive products that glowed at night with a bluish hue. Marie likened it to fairy lights.[8] In 1902, success and sadness came for Marie. After almost four years, she produced enough pure radium to convince fellow scientists that it was a real element. And her beloved father died.

A Year of Firsts

Little more than a year later, Marie had finished her research paper. That June, in front of a crowd that included her sister Bronia, Pierre and his father, and many students, scientists, and friends, Marie defended her research project. The questioning professors agreed it was a brilliant scientific achievement. Marie walked away with her PhD in physics—the first ever for a European woman.[9]

Toward the end of the year, another momentous event happened to Marie and Pierre. At first a secret committee kept the information under wraps. When the story leaked out, Pierre was taken aback. He had been nominated for the Nobel Prize in Physics along with Henri Becquerel. But

Years of hard work in a lab, such as this one, led Marie and Pierre Curie to the discovery of their second new element, radium.

The Nobel Prize

In 1903, the Nobel Prize was not very well known. The first one had been awarded only two years previously, for the discovery of X-rays. The Nobel Committee first wanted to give the award to Pierre Curie and Henri Becquerel for their work on Becquerel rays. Some committee members knew Marie's work personally, but they didn't think it proper that she be included. In the end, Marie and Pierre shared the Nobel Prize in Physics with Becquerel.

what about Marie? Pierre jumped on the news. He wrote one of the committee members explaining that Marie also deserved the award. What was the problem here? Plain and simple, many men didn't think a woman should receive the Nobel.

CHAPTER FIVE

Gone Much Too Soon

Marie and Pierre hated the fame that came with winning the Nobel Prize. Journalists and photographers hounded them. Organizations invited them to speak. Letters poured in from everywhere. Everyone wanted to know the famous couple. Fame got in the way of research. To one stunned reporter Marie said, "In science we must be interested in things, not in persons."[1]

Carrying On

Winning the Nobel Prize did have some advantages. Marie gifted some of the money to relatives and friends, had their home bathroom remodeled, and hired a lab assistant. She continued with all her duties: caring for her family, caring for the house, caring for her students, and caring for the lab. She worried about Pierre. He suffered constant aches and pains. He couldn't sleep most nights. The doctors diagnosed it as rheumatism. Marie herself was always overly tired. Did either of them think it was from radiation? One time, they talked seriously about this. Marie

Marie Curie tenderly holds the hand of her second daughter, Ève Denise.

asked what would happen if one of them suddenly died. Pierre gravely reminded her that a scientist may never abandon his work. Whatever happened, the other must go on.[2]

The Curie family soldiered on. Pierre had been promoted to professor at the Sorbonne. Marie was hired as Pierre's chief in the laboratory. This was another first—Marie's first paid job in research. On a particularly happy day in December 1904, their second daughter, Ève Denise, was born. Marie loved her girls. She tried to give Irène the attention she craved, especially after Ève came along. Pierre's father showered his affection on his granddaughters and helped around the house and garden. Through busy days and months, the Curies enjoyed the company of their few close friends and took regular summer vacations in the country. One memorable time away occurred at Easter. The family took in fresh air, picked flowers, and drank farm-fresh milk. Fourteen-month-old Ève was learning how to walk and eight-year-old Irène chased butterflies. Marie and Pierre loved this quiet getaway. None of them imagined it would be their last happy time together.

It Can't Be

Less than a week later, on April 19, 1906, Pierre Curie died. At first, Marie couldn't believe the words she was hearing. Pierre was dead. How could it be? He had left in the morning as usual. She had taken care of the girls as usual. And now he was gone?

Pierre had been crossing a busy Paris street on that rain-soaked day. Suddenly, his legs gave way, he fell, and a heavy horse cart ran him over.[3] Word of Pierre's death spread. Close friends and relatives filled the house. Overcome by grief, Marie arranged a simple burial service. She buried her husband in the cemetery at Sceaux. In Pierre's coffin, she placed his favorite picture—a photo of herself from the early days at the Sorbonne.

To Speak with Ghosts

Some believed in the ability to speak with the dead. This idea, spiritualism, was popular during the Curies' time. Pierre and Marie were not the only scientists who had been to séances, or meetings where the dead were contacted. Pierre thought it might be somehow scientific. A person, the medium, would go through certain motions and behavior to convince people that he or she was communicating with ghosts. Eventually, it was proven to be a sham.

Believers in spiritualism attended séances in the hope of communicating with the dead.

How could she go on? Marie knew she must. She waited for a few days to tell Irène. Many things changed. She hired a governess to help care for the girls. She started a journal where she wrote to Pierre, pouring out her heart as if he could understand. Later, she moved the family to a house in Sceaux.

The government of France offered to support Marie with a pension. She refused. But she did accept an offer from the Sorbonne. They asked her to take over Pierre's teaching post. What a sad way to achieve yet another first in her life—the first time a woman would teach at the Sorbonne. Marie grieved. She was grateful for the company of Pierre's father, and work at the lab kept her busy.

By November, Marie was ready to step into Pierre's shoes at the Sorbonne. She had prepared all summer for this solemn duty. The lecture hall filled to the brim. Interested onlookers crammed inside. Reporters, journalist, scientists, Pierre's former students, and Marie's students waited to hear her words. Marie's lecture began at half-past one in the afternoon, right where Pierre had left off.[4] Afterward, Marie wrote to Pierre in the journal that she lived only for his girls and old father. That was the last time she wrote to Pierre.[5]

So Much to Tackle Alone

Widowed Marie had so much to think about. She had to see to her girls' education. She had to keep teaching and working in the lab. Most of all, she had to honor Pierre's memory. She wanted to build a special laboratory. Did she think about her early experiences in Poland's Floating University? She convinced a few of her close university friends to start their own school. For a few years, Irène and eight or nine other children attended this cooperative school. They learned math, science, history, art, and literature from this group of professors and top thinkers. Marie taught science, of course.

Out of the blue, an unexpected challenge cropped up. A former colleague and famous scientist, Lord Kelvin, attacked the Curies' research. He asserted that radium was not a true element. Other scientists disagreed. With help from a long-time assistant, Marie got to work and disproved his absurd suggestion. She isolated metallic radium and calculated an accurate atomic weight.[6] Again, Marie patiently demonstrated that radium was an element.

Marie found that others also wanted to honor Pierre. A very rich American, Andrew Carnegie (1835–1919), donated $50,000 to build and support a lab dedicated to radioactivity research. This spurred the French government, the university, and the Pasteur Institute to act. Finally, Marie's wish would come true. A research lab worthy of Pierre's memory would be constructed. It would be called the Radium Institute.[7]

Struggling Against the Odds

Marie, Irène, and Ève saw it coming. Still, they weren't prepared. Dr. Curie had been Marie's dear friend and father-in-law. To Irène and Ève, he was GrandPe, their beloved grandfather. Now eighty-two, he struggled with pneumonia for almost a year, but he couldn't shake the disease. In February 1910, he died.

The next year was even stormier. Many scientists valued Marie Curie's creative thinking and research abilities. For reasons unknown, others did not. Was it jealousy? Was it a belief that women couldn't be great scientists? Whatever the reason, Marie suffered. She lost an election to the French Academy of Sciences, and she almost lost out being the first person to receive a second Nobel Prize. While at the Solvay Conference on Physics in Belgium, journalists and reporters acted like a mob. Their papers accused Marie of having a love affair and being a home wrecker. An ugly image of the physicist splashed across people's newspapers and flooded imaginations. Many thought her guilty. Marie defended herself in the papers. And she assured the Nobel Committee that her scientific achievements had nothing to do with her personal life.

CHAPTER SIX

War Changes Everything

Even though the press hounded Marie, she prevailed. On December 10, 1911, with her sister Bronia and daughter Irène watching, Marie accepted her second Nobel Prize—this time for chemistry. Curie gave a brilliant acceptance speech the next day, retelling how she and Pierre jointly discovered polonium and radium, and how she was the first person who believed radioactivity to be an atomic property. Always generous with praise, she also gave credit to many of her scientific colleagues.

Better, Bit by Bit

Exhausted, sick, and stressed from the negative press, Marie returned to Paris from Sweden. Doctors diagnosed a kidney problem. Some months later, she survived a kidney operation

This 1921 photograph shows the Curie Pavilion, or building, at the Radium Institute in Paris.

and soon left for months of rest at a secret location. Bit by bit, Marie gained strength. In November 1912, she traveled back to her homeland. A Radium Institute had been built there and she had been invited to dedicate the Warsaw facility. Russian control still dominated the area, but a visit by their world-famous, Polish-born Curie inspired and cheered up her scientific colleagues.

By the following spring, Marie felt much better. She picked up teaching at the Sorbonne again, and she planted plane trees, lime trees, and rambler roses at the Paris Radium Institute.[1] She also found time for visits with friends and family and attended the second Solvay Conference. This time, Marie and another colleague and friend, physicist Ernest Rutherford (1871–1937), spoke about an important idea: understanding atoms. For a long time, experimental work had concentrated on the structure of atoms. Rutherford said that atoms had both interior and exterior parts. Marie agreed. Later, she would describe an atom as having a nucleus surrounded by electrons.[2]

Everything on Hold

Everything hummed along until August 3, 1914. Germany and France declared war on each other, the beginning of World War I. The "Great War" soon became a global affair. The Allied powers, including French, British, Russian, and later, United States forces, fought against the Central powers, made up of armies from the Ottoman Empire, Germany, and Austria-Hungary.[3] Irène, Ève, and Marie were not together when the war broke out. The girls were vacationing on the French coast with their governess. Marie wrote telling them to be brave and that she longed to be with them. She would send for them as soon as it was safe.

As the German army neared Paris, the government left the city. Officials instructed Marie to do the same and take her supply of radium with her. She obeyed orders. Most of the

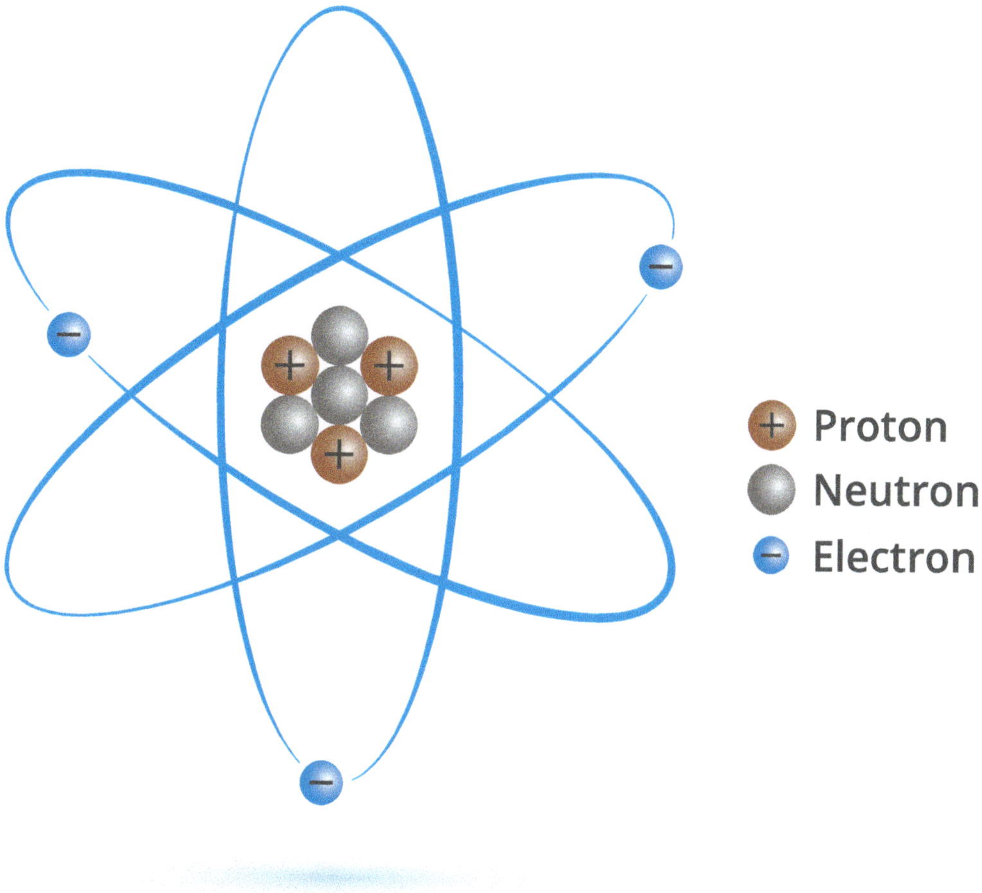

This illustration depicts the structure of an atom, with component parts of electrons, protons, and neutrons.

institute's staff had left to fight, so research was put on hold. Marie traveled by train to the coast, deposited her radium at the University of Bordeaux, and headed back to Paris. By October, the capital seemed safe from German invasion. Irène and Ève came back to the apartment to be with their mother. Irène started training to be a nurse with the Red Cross, and Ève went back to school. All of France wanted to help in the war effort, and so did the Curie family. When the government asked for donations of gold and silver, Marie didn't hesitate. She offered up assorted prize medals, including the Nobel awards. Officials refused her generous offer. Marie was determined to help. But how? She decided to turn her scientific knowledge into useful work.[4]

Marie Takes Charge

By this time in the war, many soldiers had been killed or injured. Surgeons and doctors knew that X-rays could help treat the sick and wounded. Unfortunately, not many hospitals or medical stations at the battlefront had machines or specialists offering X-ray services. That was it! Marie Curie stepped in and became director of France's Red Cross mobile radiological service. She took a crash course in anatomy and X-ray techniques. She learned how to drive a car and do basic maintenance. She convinced many wealthy people to donate money and equipment for her X-ray service. Her first "Car E" was a touring car converted into an ambulance. Its gray exterior marked with a red cross, plates painted with the French flag, and the words "Radiologic Service" identified the vehicle as Marie's first mobile

In 1914, Marie eagerly drove to different locations with her mobile X-ray service vehicle. She wanted to do her part for the war effort.

car. Others followed, nicknamed the "Little Curies." Her very first call came on November 1, 1914. Off she went at a whopping 20 miles (32 kilometers) per hour.[5] After that, requests for help by telegram or telephone came in constantly.

Seventeen-year-old Irène assisted her mother for many of these emergency calls. The two worked together as a team to unload and set up equipment and reassure wounded soldiers. Sometimes, they even had to convince doctors that the X-rays could locate broken bones or bullets inside patients. Before long, Marie put Irène in charge of a hospital unit. This daughter of scientists shone. She expertly set up equipment and took X-rays of the injured. Irène also assisted in surgeries. Marie Curie's scientific friends also helped the war effort. Two of them used their knowledge of physics and sound to invent sonar-like detection systems. Because of this, underwater enemy submarines or planes hiding among cloud-filled skies could be better seen. Others served as hospital directors and nurses.

Despite being extremely busy, Marie and her girls had time for other things. Marie spent time at the Radium Institute training nurses and everyday citizens as X-ray technicians. Irène and Ève attended classes as often as they could, and they knitted sweaters for soldiers. Marie also collected flower and herb seeds here and there. She and Irène later planted them in the institute's garden. By 1918, Paris had been attacked several times. In July, it happened again, and thankfully the Allied armies pushed the enemy away once more. Irène received her science degree in physics and began thinking about what to do for advanced research.

Everyone the world over hoped and prayed for peace. At eleven in the morning on November 11, 1918, cannon fire erupted in Paris. It signaled the end of the Great War. Marie Curie's twenty "Little Curies" along with two hundred outfitted X-ray rooms had examined over a million soldiers.[6] Thousands of

Treaty After War

By January 1919, the Paris Peace Conference began. Meeting in Versailles, it would establish the terms of peace. Thirty nations came, but only four took on large roles—the United Kingdom, France, Italy, and the United States. The Treaty of Versailles included an agreement to form the League of Nations, which many believed would prevent future wars. Germany, however, felt it was treated too harshly by the treaty.

those wounded survived as a result. In appreciation, France gave Irène a military medal commemorating her service. Her mother got nothing.[7] But Marie Curie probably didn't mind. She received a better reward. She saw her native country lifted from under the weight of Russian control. With the end of the war, Poland became its own nation once more. Poles were free to speak their language, practice their culture, and live unafraid.

CHAPTER SEVEN

Coming Back After the War

After the war ended, Marie was anxious to get the Radium Institute up to full speed. Half of the building, the Curie Pavilion, was under Marie's supervision, and it was a laboratory devoted to research in physics and chemistry.[1] It didn't hum with research and workers—yet. The other half, the Pasteur Pavilion, fell under the direction of Dr. Claudius Regaud and specialized in the biological effects and medical applications of radioactivity.[2] The street in front of it was named after Pierre Curie.

A Start

As she had throughout her life, Marie Curie wasted no time. By the spring of 1919, she extended her X-ray class instruction to American army officers. These service persons wished to become technicians able to administer life-saving

Marie Curie (*seated*) and her daughter Irène (*standing right of center*) trained Americans at the Radium Institute following the end of the war.

X-ray techniques when they got back home. It was a good thing for Marie. She had lost most of her money donating to France for war bonds and now was almost poor herself.[3] Luckily, the US Army paid her seventy-five dollars a week to teach the energetic technician recruits.[4]

The following year, a wealthy Frenchman gave money to start the Curie Foundation. Henri de Rothschild (1872–1947) believed in scientific research. Although a doctor himself, he didn't practice medicine. His generous donation boosted Marie's lab. With it, she staffed her lab with many industrious researchers. Both labs of the institute collaborated. Treating diseases, especially cancer, became the common goal. Because of this, radium was in constant demand. Hospitals, doctors, labs, businesses, and entrepreneurs around the world clamored for more of the radioactive material. Who had the precious matter? Not the institute on Pierre Curie Street. Both Marie and Irène were eager to expand their research. And their tiny one-gram amount of radium, about as much as a thimbleful, simply wasn't enough.[5]

Dealing with the Press Again

Marie mustered courage. She had to increase the institute's monetary support. Where would she turn? Marie would have to deal with journalists and newspapers again—this time the American press. A New York editor, Marie Mattingly Meloney (1878–1943), came to call. "Missy" Meloney edited a popular women's magazine, the *Delineator*. Short, gray-haired, and walking with a slight limp, the editor sought an interview with Marie. Meloney wrote to the famous scientist, her idol, saying that she'd been admiring Marie's work for twenty years. Could Marie trust this American? She took a chance.

Meloney didn't expect what she saw. A small woman in a black dress welcomed her into an office. Meloney later wrote that Marie had the saddest expression that she had ever seen. It was hard for Meloney to begin, but she explained to Marie that women all over America were interested in her work. How did Marie feel? She launched into an explanation. The United States had almost fifty grams of radium, including seven in New York, six in Denver, and four in Baltimore.[6] Meloney listened with interest and then asked Marie how much she had. Marie answered. *She* did not have any, but her lab had about one gram. Meloney was shocked. She asked Marie about the money she received from patents on radium. Did Marie sigh? Perhaps. But Marie probably thought back to the conversation she and Pierre had had a long time ago. They both decided not to patent their discovery of radium and the processes needed to produce it. They agreed that the new element was a gift to the world and didn't belong to them. So no, Marie did not have patents on radium, which could have earned money for her lab.[7]

Whirlwind Missy

Missy Meloney jumped into action, much like Marie had always done. She knew that one gram of radium would cost at least $100,000. An enormous amount of money! Meloney first asked several rich women to donate to her cause. They didn't part with their cash. She turned to her readers. Surely, they would give to Marie Curie. Not surprisingly, women from all over sent donations. Even children mailed nickels and dimes to the Curie fund.[8] It wasn't long before Meloney reached her goal.

Fifty-three-year-old Curie agreed to come to America. Marie knew she had to graciously accept the radium purchased in her name. On May 4, 1921, Marie, Irène, and Ève set sail for New York. When they arrived later in the month, hordes of well-wishers lined the dock. Reporters, Polish Americans, Girl Scouts, scientists, everyday people: they all wanted to welcome the Curies. A whirlwind of activities awaited. Colleges wanted to grant honorary degrees, students wanted to hear from the great scientist, and countless other organizations and businesses wanted to show off to Marie. To top it off, President Warren G. Harding presented Curie with the box containing a precious gram of radium (the box originally was empty but was filled before Marie went back to France).

(*From left to right*) Missy Meloney, Irène, Marie, and Ève pose for this picture, taken when the Curies visited America in 1921.

Another Great Scientist

Ernest Rutherford was a great scientist and a friend and colleague of Marie Curie's. Rutherford used radiation to discover what was inside atoms. A big part of his efforts showed that protons and neutrons make up the nucleus of the atom. He also discovered that when atoms radioactively decay, they change from one element to another.

Marie's US tour continued. At times, she was so tired that Irène and Ève took her place at some of the scheduled events. The girls loved every minute. Sometimes, they even got to have fun playing tennis, boating, swimming, or enjoying an amusement park. The three Curies eventually saw the Grand Canyon and Niagara Falls before returning to France in July. Marie returned home with a bounty: the radium, other valuable minerals, extra cash, and a contract to write a book.

Back in Charge at the Institute

Marie had her radium and extra money to improve research conditions at the Radium Institute. A pleasant surprise came up the next winter. The Paris Academy of Medicine voted to have her as a new member. It was the first time in more than two hundred years that the male-only-member tradition was broken. Marie accepted.

Irène and Ève were well on their way in life. Irène edged toward a career in her parents' footsteps. She would soon complete her own research under her mother's guidance and be awarded a doctorate in physics. Eventually, Irène married another scientist, Frédéric Joliot (1900–1958), from her mother's lab.

Irène and Frédéric became scientific partners, much like Marie and Pierre. Ève took a completely different direction. She became the artist of the family. When a career as a concert pianist didn't pan out, Ève picked up on her talent for writing. She eventually completed a much-admired biography of her own mother.

When able, Marie traveled to promote science. She wished her lab to continue after her death, for Irène, Frédéric, and all the other remarkable scientists working there. She made a second trip to the United States to drum up financial support for the Radium Institute in Warsaw. And in 1932, Marie dedicated the Polish Institute. It was the last time she would see her beloved homeland. Her health continued to deteriorate, and on July 4, 1934, sixty-six-year-old Marie Sklodowska Curie died.

Conclusion

Getting X-rays before a dental procedure. Heating up a morning cup of coffee. Having diagnostic work done in an MRI machine before surgery. Eating food that is bacteria-free. All these common everyday occurrences are possible because of the science of radiation. Radioactivity happens when atoms of radioactive substances release radiation. This information had not always been known.

Marie Sklodowska Curie and Pierre Curie were great scientists. They shared a life dedicated to education and science. They saw scientific discovery as something to benefit the world. They met, found they had much in common, married, and formed a partnership of equals. This partnership encountered many ups and downs. Especially challenging was the common notion of the time that women belonged at home, taking care of their families. Women were believed to be incapable of doing great work, especially in science. Marie would prove all the doubters wrong.

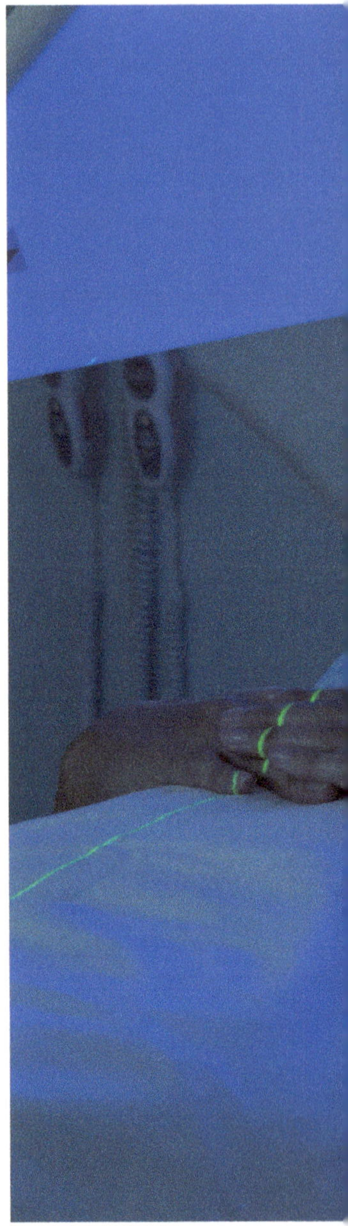

At first, Marie and Pierre worked on separate scientific issues. Sparks flew when they teamed up to study newly found mysterious and energetic rays. They discovered new elements and changed the way science thought about atoms. Marie coined the terms "radioactive" and "radioactivity" to explain their new science.

Unfortunately for herself, her daughters, her father-in-law, friends, and the world at large, this great scientific pairing ended abruptly and much too soon. Sure, the Curies had already received the Nobel Prize for their first big project. But most likely the famous pair would have continued working together, making dynamite discoveries. Marie was shaken by Pierre's death but managed to soldier on. She took care of her daughters as best she could, making sure they had an excellent education.

Marie marched ahead with the rest of the scientific world. New discoveries by many other scientists built upon the Curies' earlier work. Scientific conferences brought great minds such as Albert Einstein and Ernest Rutherford together to listen to and learn from each other. Radiation, radioactivity, energy, and the structure of the atom were all topics that were debated and discussed.

Eventually, Marie and Pierre's own daughter Irène carried on the tradition of her parents. She and her husband Frédéric became another celebrated couple in physical science. They,

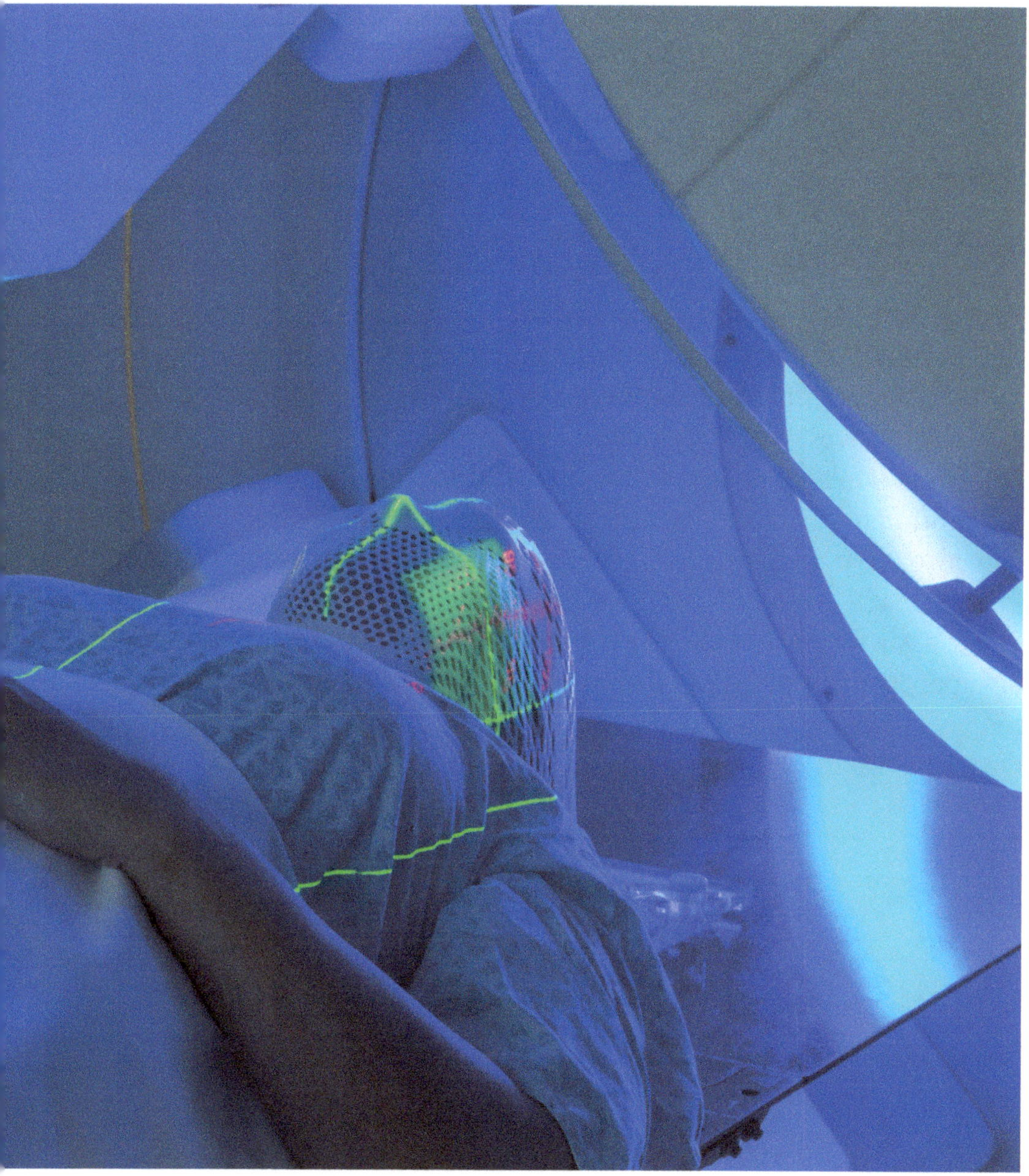

Radiation is a common form of treatment for some of today's illnesses. This person undergoes radiation therapy.

too, would be awarded a Nobel Prize. At first, the dangers of radiation were not well known. It is true that Pierre had made early discoveries about potential problems. But for some reason, the positives about radiation were emphasized and even exaggerated. Later, the negative consequences surrounding radiation and radioactivity were firmly established.

The discoveries by Marie and Pierre, along with the scientists working before, during, and after them, ushered in the use of radiation in medicine and the atomic age. Today, radiation and radioactive materials are everywhere. They are found in batteries, microwaves, and food. They are used in medical and dental procedures. Scientists know that matter converts itself to energy and can calculate the time it takes for radioactive elements to lose their radiant force. And of course, countries can obtain radioactive energy and possess extremely destructive power.

All this is because two young scientists met, married, and became one of history's most dynamic scientific teams.

CHRONOLOGY

- **1859** Pierre Currie is born in Paris, France, on May 15.
- **1867** Maria "Marie" Salomea Sklodowska is born in Warsaw, Poland, on November 7.
- **1883** Marie graduates from high school, finishing first in her class.
- **1891** Marie moves to Paris and begins college at the Sorbonne.
- **1894** Pierre and Marie meet in spring. Marie already has her first degree and is about to graduate with her second.
- **1895** Marie and Pierre get married in the summer.
- **1897** Irène, the first child of Marie and Pierre, is born on September 12.
- **1898** The Curies announce their discovery of polonium, and soon after, radium.
- **1903** Marie becomes the first woman to earn a PhD from the Sorbonne; the Curies are awarded the Nobel Prize in Physics.
- **1904** Ève, the second child of Marie and Pierre, is born on December 6.
- **1906** On April 19, Pierre is killed in an accident; Marie takes over for him as professor at the Sorbonne.
- **1909** Plans are in the works to build the Radium Institute.
- **1910** Pierre's father, Dr. Eugène Curie, dies after a long bout of pneumonia.
- **1911** Marie is harassed by newspapers and journalists; she is awarded her second Nobel Prize, this one in Chemistry.
- **1914** World War I starts; Marie begins her radiologic work.
- **1921** Marie and her daughters travel to the United States to receive radium donated by American women.

- **1934** Irène and Frédéric Joliot discover artificial radioactivity; Marie dies on July 4, and doctors say it is from repeated exposure to radiation.
- **1935** Irène shares the Nobel Prize in Chemistry with her husband for the discovery of artificial radioactivity.
- **1995** The coffins of both Pierre and Marie Curie are moved to the Pantheon in Paris.

CHAPTER NOTES

Introduction

1. Tim Lambert, "A History of Science and Technology in the 19th Century," A World History Encyclopedia, http://www.localhistories.org/victech.html (accessed April 27, 2019).

Chapter One The Early Years

1. Ève Curie, *Madame Curie* (New York: Doubleday & Co., 1937), p. 9.
2. Susan Quinn, *Marie Curie* (New York: Simon & Schuster, 1995), p. 17.
3. "The Three Partitions, 1764-95," Glenn E. Curtis, ed., *Poland: A Country Study* (Washington, DC: GPO for the Library of Congress, 1992), http://countrystudies.us/poland/11.htm.
4. Quinn, p. 28.
5. Ève Curie, pp. 15–16.
6. Ève Curie, pp. 18–19.
7. Marie Curie, *Pierre Curie* (New York: Dover Publications, 1963), p.14.
8. Denis Brian, *The Curies: A Biography of the Most Controversial Family in Science* (Hoboken, NJ: John Wiley & Sons, 2005), pp. 4–6.
9. Brian, p. 4.
10. Marie Curie, p. 15; Brian, p. 6.

Chapter Two Young Scientists

1. Susan Quinn, *Marie Curie* (New York: Simon & Schuster, 1995), p. 52.
2. Quinn, pp. 56–58.
3. Quinn, pp. 56–58; Ève Curie, *Madame Curie* (New York: Doubleday & Co., 1937), pp. 42–43.
4. Curie, p. 53.
5. Curie, p. 90.
6. Denis Brian, *The Curies: A Biography of the Most Controversial Family in Science* (Hoboken, NJ: John Wiley & Sons, 2005), pp. 11–12.

7. Brian, pp. 13–15.

Chapter Three Together at Last

1. Susan Quinn, *Marie Curie* (New York: Simon & Schuster, 1995), p. 115.
2. American Institute of Physics, "A Student in Paris," Marie Curie and the Science of Radioactivity, https://history.aip.org/history/exhibits/curie/stud1.htm (accessed April 27, 2019).
3. Ève Curie, *Madame Curie* (New York: Doubleday & Co., 1937), pp. 121–122.
4. Quinn, p. 124.
5. American Institute of Physics, "A Student in Paris."
6. American Institute of Physics, "Research Breakthroughs," Marie Curie and the Science of Radioactivity, https://history.aip.org/history/exhibits/curie/resbr1.htm (accessed April 27, 2019).

Chapter Four Radioactive

1. American Institute of Physics, "Research Breakthroughs," Marie Curie and the Science of Radioactivity, https://history.aip.org/history/exhibits/curie/resbr1.htm (accessed April 27, 2019).
2. Ève Curie, *Madame Curie* (New York: Doubleday & Co., 1937), p. 155.
3. Susan Quinn, *Marie Curie* (New York: Simon & Schuster, 1995), p. 146.
4. American Institute of Physics, "Marie Curie in Her Own Words," Marie Curie and the Science of Radioactivity, https://history.aip.org/history/exhibits/curie/brief/06_quotes/quotes_07.html (accessed April 27, 2019).
5. Denis Brian, *The Curies: A Biography of the Most Controversial Family in Science* (Hoboken, NJ: John Wiley & Sons, 2005), p. 57.
6. Brian, pp. 57–59; Quinn, pp. 149–152.

7. Brian, p. 60.
8. American Institute of Physics, "Research Breakthroughs."
9. Mary Bagley, "Marie Curie: Facts & Biography," LiveScience, August 14, 2013, https://www.livescience.com/38907-marie-curie-facts-biography.html.

Chapter Five Gone Much Too Soon

1. Ève Curie, *Madame Curie* (New York: Doubleday & Co., 1937), p. 222.
2. Ève Curie, pp. 191–192; Marie Curie, *Pierre Curie* (New York: Dover Publications, 1963), p. 94.
3. Ève Curie, p. 253.
4. Ève Curie, p. 258.
5. Denis Brian, *The Curies: A Biography of the Most Controversial Family in Science* (Hoboken, NJ: John Wiley & Sons, 2005), p. 108.
6. Marie Curie, *Pierre Curie* (New York: Dover Publications, 1963), p. 97.
7. Brian, p. 113.

Chapter Six War Changes Everything

1. Ève Curie, *Madame Curie* (New York: Doubleday & Co., 1937), p. 286.
2. Denis Brian, *The Curies: A Biography of the Most Controversial Family in Science* (Hoboken, NJ: John Wiley & Sons, 2005), p. 154.
3. Carly-Sue, "August 3, 1914 CE: France and Germany Declare War," *National Geographic,* updated July 7, 2014, https://www.nationalgeographic.org/thisday/aug3/france-and-germany-declare-war.
4. Marie Curie, *Pierre Curie* (New York: Dover Publications, 1963), pp. 102–103.
5. Denis Brian, *The Curies: A Biography of the Most Controversial Family in Science* (Hoboken, NJ: John Wiley & Sons, 2005), p. 161.

6. Ève Curie, p. 297.
7. Brian, p. 169.

Chapter Seven Coming Back After the War

1. Nathalie Oudar, "Our History," Institut Curie, May 30, 2017, https://institut-curie.org/page/our-history.
2. Oudar.
3. Ève Curie, *Madame Curie* (New York: Doubleday & Co., 1937), p. 305.
4. Denis Brian, *The Curies: A Biography of the Most Controversial Family in Science* (Hoboken, NJ: John Wiley & Sons, 2005), p. 172.
5. Brian, p. 173.
6. Curie, p. 323.
7. Curie, pp. 203–204.
8. Brian, p. 176.

GLOSSARY

atom The smallest particle of an element, consisting of protons, neutrons, and electrons.

atomic weight The mass of an atom.

Becquerel rays Energy, first observed by Henri Becquerel, given off by radioactive substances such as uranium and radium.

electrometer An instrument invented by Pierre Curie to measure faint electrical currents.

electroscope An instrument used for science experiments at this time.

element A substance that is made up of atoms and exists in nature, such as argon, hydrogen, polonium, and radium.

EPCI The School of Industrial Physics and Chemistry, where Pierre Curie worked.

fairy lights Another name for Christmas lights; lights that can be strung up around a room that seem to twinkle like fairies.

headmistress A woman in charge of a school.

ionize To make a substance, such as air or water, a conductor of electricity.

patent A document that proves ownership of an invention.

piezoelectricity Scientific laws discovered about crystals by Pierre Curie.

pitchblende A brownish mineral ore made up of many different elements.

polonium A new radioactive element discovered by Marie and Pierre Curie.

radioactive Having to do with a substance that gives off rays.

radioactivity The ability of an atom to release radiation.

radiological Having to do with X-ray treatment.

radium The second new radioactive element found by the Curies.

Sorbonne A university in Paris.

triton A type of snail that lives in the water.

FURTHER READING

BOOKS

Bodden, Valerie. *Marie Curie: Chemist and Physicist.* Minneapolis, MN: Essential Library, 2018.

Conkling, Winifred. *Radioactive! How Irène Curie and Lise Meitner Revolutionized Science and Changed the World.* Chapel Hill, NC: Algonquin Young Readers, 2018.

Ethridge, Maggie May. *Marie Curie: Radioactivity Pioneer and the First Woman to Win a Nobel Prize.* New York: Cavendish Square, 2017.

Milani, Alice. *Marie Curie: A Life of Discovery.* Minneapolis, MN: Graphic Universe, 2019.

WEBSITES

Atomic Heritage Foundation
atomicheritage.org/search/all/Marie%20Curie
Discover more about the Curie family of scientists and other important people in the race to the atomic age.

Marie Curie and the Science of Radioactivity
history.aip.org/exhibits/curie/
Learn more about Pierre and Marie Curie and their scientific discoveries.

Smithsonian.com
smithsonianmag.com/history/how-marie-curie-brought-x-ray-machines-to-battlefield-180965240/
Read about Marie Curie's exploits as a mobile X-ray technician and how she heroically saved many lives during World War I.

INDEX